This library edition published in 2011 by Walter Foster Publishing, Inc.
Walter Foster Library
Distributed by Black Rabbit Books.
P.O. Box 3263 Mankato, Minnesota 56002

Printed in China by CT PRINTING, Shenzhen.

First Library Edition

Library of Congress Cataloging-in-Publication Data

Learn to draw The fairies of Pixie Hollow / illustrated by the Disney Storybook Artists. -- 1st library ed.
     p. cm.
  ISBN 978-1-936309-05-4 (hardcover)
  1. Cartoon characters. 2. Drawing--Technique. 3. Fairies in art. I. Disney Storybook Artists. II. Title: Fairies of Pixie Hollow.
  NC1764.L353 2011
  741.5'1--dc22

                                                    2010005329

022010
0P1816

9 8 7 6 5 4 3 2 1

Disney Fairies

Learn to Draw
The Fairies of
Pixie Hollow

Deep in the heart of the magical island of Never Land there is an enchanted place called Pixie Hollow. Here tiny fairies—each with a special talent—live, work, and play. When you turn the page, you'll learn more about these fairies—and you'll also learn how to re-create the fairies in their magical miniature world!

Illustrated by the Disney Storybook Artists

Getting Started

Tools and Materials

You don't need to be an art-talent fairy to draw the residents of Pixie Hollow, but you will need to gather a few simple drawing tools. Start with a regular pencil so you easily can erase any mistakes. Make sure to have an eraser and a sharpener too. When you're done with a drawing, you can add color with markers, crayons, colored pencils, or even watercolors. The choice is up to you!

colored pencils

drawing pencil

markers

eraser

sharpener

paintbrush and paints

How to Use This Book

You can draw any fairy by following the simple steps in this book. You'll be amazed at how fun and easy it is!

Step 1

Start your drawing in the middle of the paper so you won't run out of room.

Step 2

Each new step appears in blue, so draw all the blue lines you see.

Step 3

Refine the lines of your drawing. Then add the details.

Step 4

Darken the lines you want to keep, and erase the rest.

Step 5

Use beautiful, enchanting colors to make your drawing come alive!

3

Tinker Bell

Tinker Bell is the most famous fairy—thanks to Peter Pan! Tink and Peter were once best friends, until she returned to live with the rest of the fairies in Pixie Hollow. Now Tinker Bell spends most of her time tinkering inside her teakettle workshop. She is hands-down the best pots-and-pans fairy in Pixie Hollow. She's also brave, loyal, and protective—a true friend!

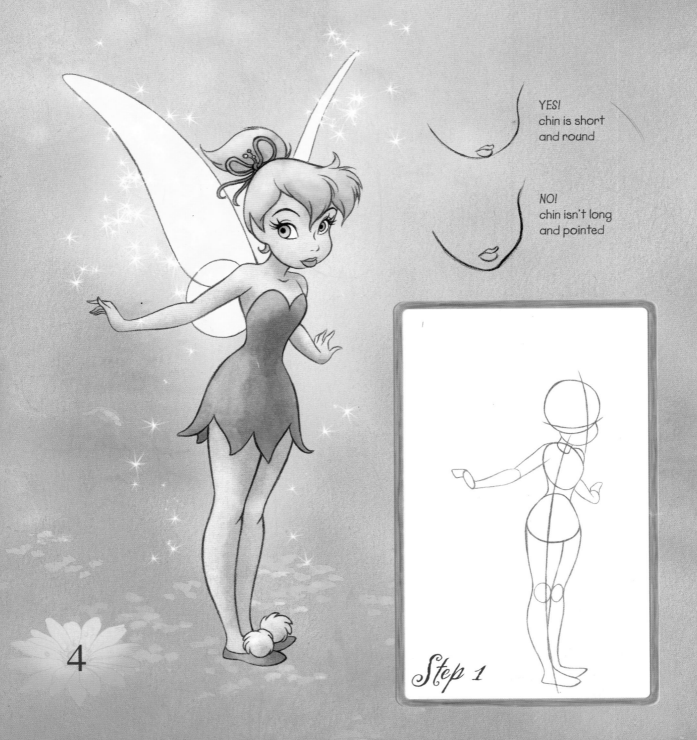

YES!
chin is short
and round

NO!
chin isn't long
and pointed

Step 1

Step 2

YES!
eyes are set
at an angle

NO!
not set on a
straight line

YES!
ear is pointed

NO!
not round

Step 3

YES!
Tink's nose turns
up slightly

NO!
not downturned

NO!
not too far
up in the air

Step 4

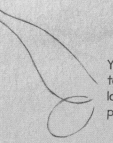

YES!
top wing is
long and
pointed

NO!
not short
and oval, like
bottom wing

5

Rani Portrait

As a water-talent fairy, Rani can do amazing, magical things with water. She can shape it into a ball or pick it up in her bare hands—without spilling a drop! Like most water fairies, Rani is full of water herself, so she cries more easily than fairies from other talents. But she's quick to smile or laugh too! Of all the water-talent fairies, Rani loves water the most.

Step 1

YES!
lips are small with
thin upper lip

NO!
not plump like this

Step 2

Step 3

YES!
headband has fluid, smooth shapes, like water drops

NO!
not stiff and pointed

Step 4

YES!
Rani's eyes are angled upward

NO!
not set horizontally

7

Rani

Rani is the only fairy without wings, so she can't fly without the help of her bird friend, Brother Dove. But Rani isn't too upset about being wingless, because it means she can swim—something that fairies with wings can't do! Rani's moods flow like water—she's impulsive and emotional. But Rani also has an inner strength that serves her well.

YES!
sleeve is loose
and flowing

NO!
not stiff and
starched looking

Step 1

Step 2

Step 3

YES!
hair is thick
and loose

NO!
not flat and
tight against
the skull

Step 4

pouches are
shaped like hearts

Beck Portrait

Beck is one of the most gifted animal-talent fairies. She can speak to any animal in its own language, whether it's Bird, Chipmunk, or even Porcupine! She also can sense how an animal is feeling, instantly knowing if it is happy, scared, or angry. Beck is a bit shy. She's more comfortable with animals than with her fellow fairies—and sometimes she secretly wishes she were an animal herself.

YES!
eyes have a
few individual
lashes

NO!
not one
thick lash

NO!
not a lot of
long lashes

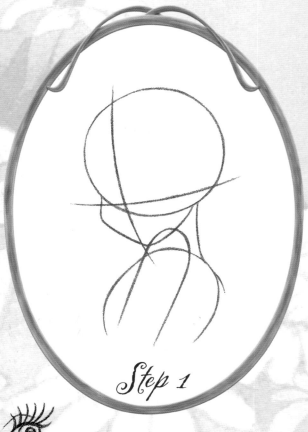

Step 1

Beck wears her
hair in braids

YES!
loose and
simple

NO!
not tight and
detailed

Step 2

Step 3

Beck wears an armband
on her upper left arm

YES!
follows shape
of arm

NO!
not flat and
shapeless
like this

Step 4

YES!
upper lip is thinner
than bottom lip

NO!
upper lip is not full

11

Beck

Like the animals she spends time with, Beck has a curious and playful nature. She loves to play games with insects, and her adventurous spirit often leads her to discover exciting new places. But Beck also has a practical side. When the animals have disagreements, kind-hearted, sensible Beck is the one who acts as the go-between to bring back peace to the animal kingdom!

Beck's hat is made from a leaf and topped with a berry

Step 1

Step 2

Step 3

Step 4

YES!
leaf skirt is soft
and flexible

NO!
not stiff with
jagged edges

Beck's vest is made of
two leaves, stitched
together at sides,
with berries at
shoulders

13

Fira Portrait

The most talented of the light-talent fairies, Fira can single-handedly light the entire Home Tree with her glow. Fira's personality is a match for her talent—she's bright and fiery! She also has a radiant charm and charisma that attracts other light fairies, who look to her for advice—making Fira a natural-born leader.

Step 1

YES!
hair is soft and
simple with wavy lines

NO!
not too much detail
or too many lines

14

Step 2

Step 3

Step 4

YES!
eyelashes are
thick and eyebrow
is tapered

NO!
lashes and brow
aren't thin

NO!
eyebrow is
not thick

YES!
upper lip comes to
point at the center

NO!
lip doesn't indent
like this

Fira

Fira uses her light talent to train the fireflies that light Pixie Hollow at night. And she also stars in the fairies' light show! But glowing so brightly takes up a lot of energy. To refuel, Fira naps in the bright light of the sun. Fira's closest friends nicknamed her Moth, because they say she is drawn to light like a moth to a flame!

YES!
belt is soft with
smooth edges

NO!
not jagged
and sharp

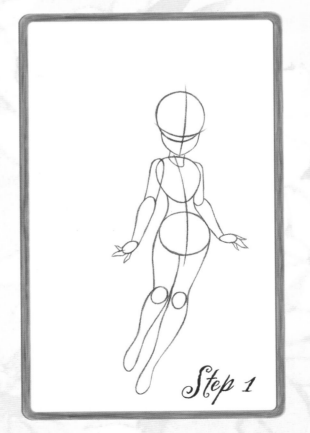

Step 1

Step 2

Step 3

YES!
wings are curved
and rounded

NO!
not stiff with
sharp edges

Step 4

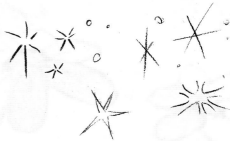

Fira is surrounded by
light effects of varying
shapes and sizes—just
like pixie dust!

17

Vidia Portrait

Vidia is the fastest fast-flying-talent fairy in all of Pixie Hollow. She is also the most selfish! Vidia lives alone, away from the rest of the fairies, in a sour-plum tree. And Vidia rarely has anything kind to say to anyone.

YES!
lips are
angular

NO!
not rounded
and smooth

Step 1

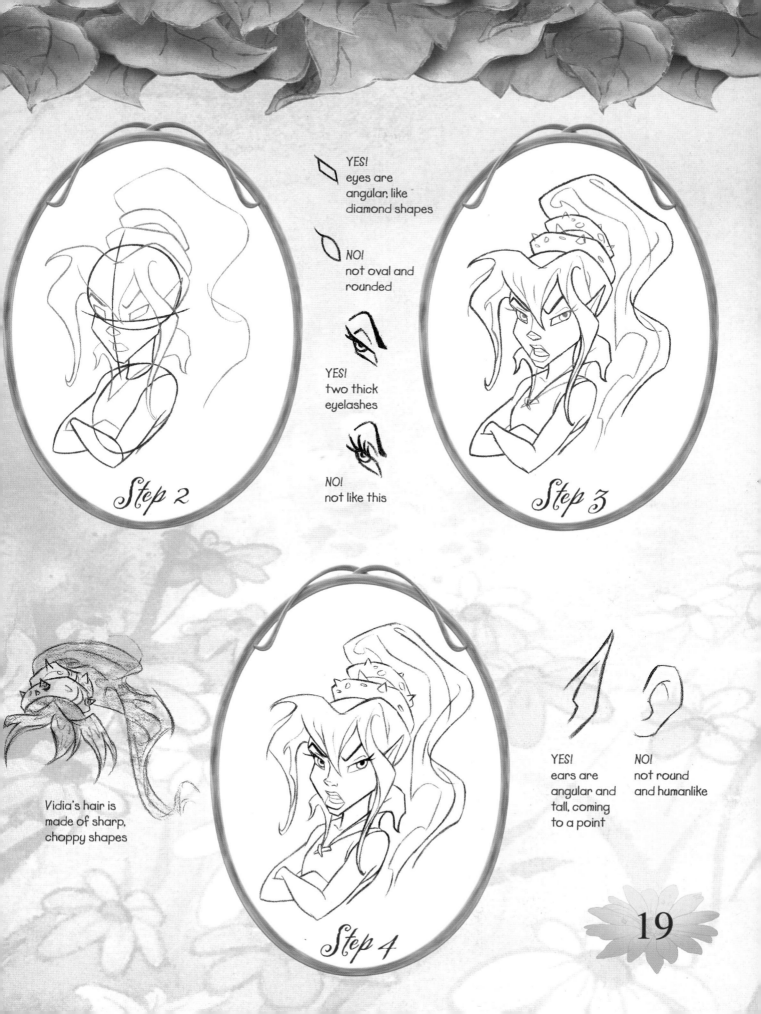

YES!
eyes are angular, like diamond shapes

NO!
not oval and rounded

YES!
two thick eyelashes

NO!
not like this

Step 2

Step 3

Vidia's hair is made of sharp, choppy shapes

Step 4

YES!
ears are angular and tall, coming to a point

NO!
not round and humanlike

19

Vidia

Vidia is well known among the fairies for her nasty attitude and her selfish behavior. She's always making trouble—and she couldn't care less what the rest of the fairies think of her. Yet Vidia is still a part of the fairy kingdom. When push comes to shove, she'll come to the aid of her fellow fairies—even if she does so begrudgingly and with a sour temper!

YES!
Vidia's hair tie is a thick blackberry vine with large, sharp thorns

NO!
vine isn't thin like this

Step 1

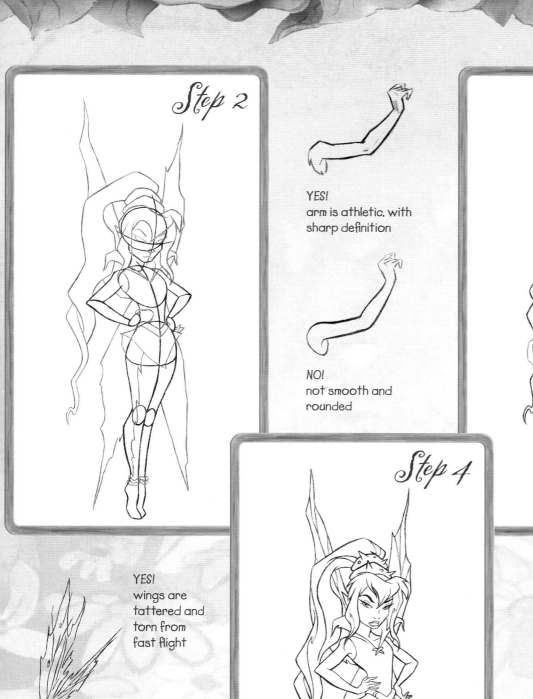

Step 2

YES!
arm is athletic, with
sharp definition

NO!
not smooth and
rounded

Step 3

Step 4

YES!
wings are
tattered and
torn from
fast flight

NO!
not fresh
and stiff

everything about Vidia
is sharp and angular,
including her leaf skirt

21

Prilla

Prilla is truly one of a kind: She's the first and only clapping-talent fairy that Pixie Hollow has ever seen! She's also the only fairy who can transport herself to the mainland at will. In the blink of an eye, she can visit with human children and, if necessary, persuade them to clap to save a fairy. Prilla's talent is very important. By keeping up children's belief in fairies, she saves many fairies' lives!

YES!
seedpod hat is simple,
with few details

NO!
not detailed
like this

Step 1

Step 2

YES!
flower petal
underskirt is fluid
with curled edges

NO!
not stiff with
perfect edges

Step 3

YES!
wings are fluid,
graceful, and
flowing

NO!
not stiff
and rigid

NO!
not
featherlike

Step 4

YES!
edges of leaf
apron are
irregular

NO!
apron isn't
stiff with
defined edges

23

Lily

A very skilled garden-talent fairy, Lily is practical, generous, and patient. With her friendly smile and sparkling eyes, she's as fresh and lovely as the flowers she tends! Lily treasures all plants, and she communicates with them in almost the same way that Beck interacts with animals—she can sense if they feel happy, troubled, or in danger.

Lily's hat is a flower with curled-up petals

Step 1

Step 2

YES!
indent in center
of top lip

NO!
not pointed
in center like
Fira's lips

YES!
eye shape like
a petal coming
to a point

NO!
too balanced,
rounded

Step 3

YES!
bow is tied
at the side

NO!
not tied under
her chin

Step 4

YES!
leggings end in
irregular petal
shapes

NO!
edges aren't stiff
and cloudlike

25

Bess

Bess is well known as the most gifted art-talent fairy. She finds artistic inspiration in everything, so she easily becomes distracted by colors and interesting forms. Bess gets so involved in her artwork that she often doesn't notice the paint spatters on her clothes! She never tires of hearing praise for her work, but she's very sensitive to criticism.

YES!
art-talent fairy
has a well-used
brush with
twig handle

NO!
not fresh and
stiff like new
brushes from
the art store

Step 1

Step 2

Bess wears a flower on her ponytail

YES! petals vary and overlap

NO! not flat and symmetrical

YES! leggings have rounded, irregular ruffles

NO! not even and regular like these

Step 3

YES! wings have oval design

NO! not veinlike lines

Step 4

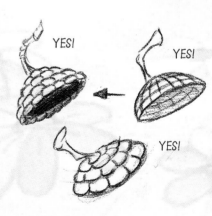

YES!   **YES!**

YES!

Bess's cap follows a curved shape, and pattern wraps around the hat

27

Terence

Terence's personality isn't the only thing that glitters. As a pixie-dust-talent sparrow man, he spends his days measuring and distributing the fairy dust that enables Never Land's fairies to fly and do their magic. And the glittering dust sticks with Terence long after his work is done, enhancing his sparkling smile.

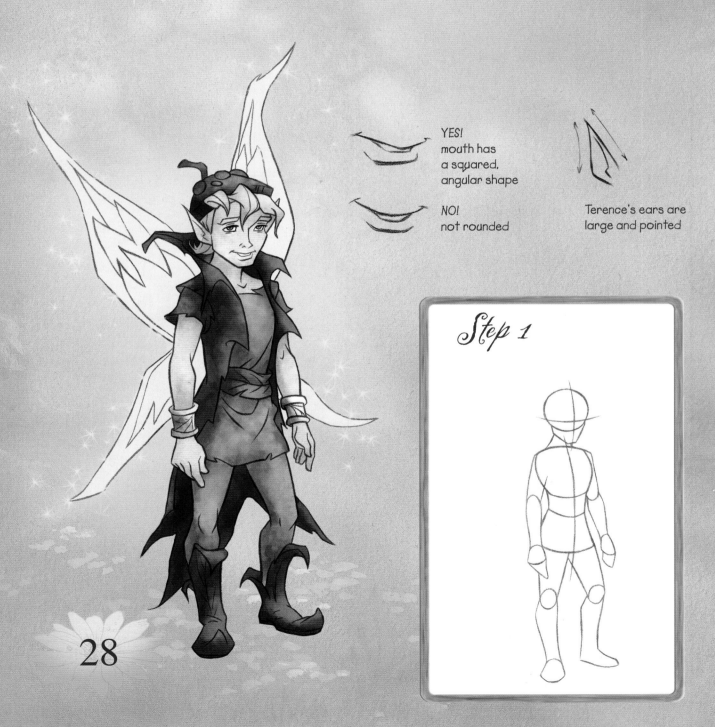

YES!
mouth has
a squared,
angular shape

NO!
not rounded

Terence's ears are
large and pointed

Step 1

Step 2

YES!
bumps on hat
are raised
and rounded

NO!
not flat and
smooth

Step 3

YES!
nose has
sharp angles

NO!
not sloped and
smooth

NO!
not straight and
shapeless

Step 4

YES!
hand is large
and strong
with square
fingertips

NO!
not thin with tapered
fingertips

29

Queen Clarion

The dignified, supremely noble ruler of Pixie Hollow, Queen Clarion is warm, wise, fair, and compassionate—everything you'd want in a ruler. She chooses her words with a caution and thoughtfulness that command respect and honesty from all. It's no wonder the other fairies love their elegant queen so much!

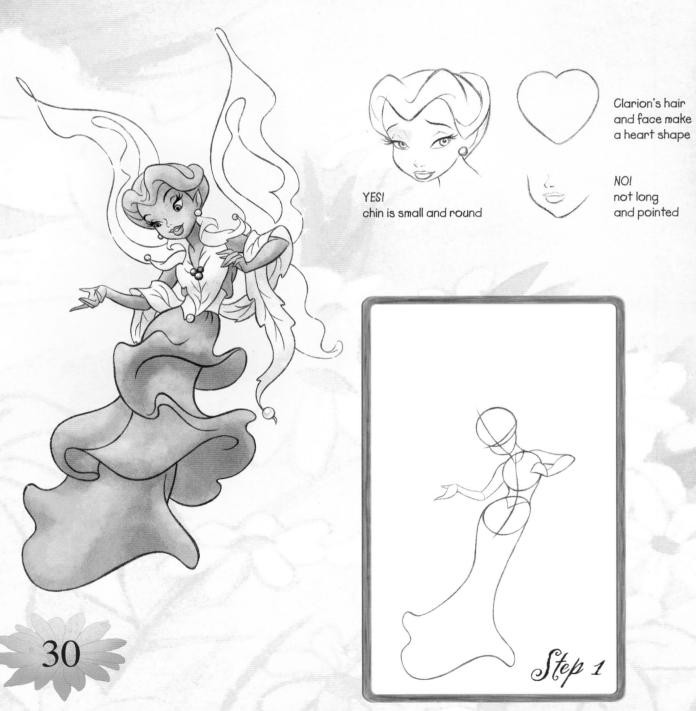

YES!
chin is small and round

Clarion's hair and face make a heart shape

NO!
not long and pointed

Step 1

Step 2

YES!
eyes are
small and set
at an angle

NO!
not large
and straight

Step 3

Queen Clarion's wings have a
natural looseness and delicacy

Step 4

NO!
wings are
not scalloped

NO!
not pointed

Thanks for visiting . . .

Now when you hear the tinkling of bells, you'll know you're not far from the Home Tree and the magical, enchanted world of the talented fairies you've come to know—and draw—so well!

Believing is just the beginning!